P9-CIS-127

TO SCOTT Sm

FROM

Stephen Richey

12-7-09

The Galley

by

Stephen Richey

First published by Dog Ear Publishing
4010 W. 86th Street, Ste H
Indianapolis, IN 46268
www.dogearpublishing.net

ISBN: 978-159858-426-4

This book is printed on acid-free paper.

Printed in the United States of America

Illustrations by Eric Malabanan

Prologue to "The Galley"

I'd been in construction in California for nearly thirty years. I'd just been laid off by the third house builder/land developer I had worked for over the years to go bankrupt. When their houses of cards crumble, everyone they employ, no longer has a job.

I was out of work with no income coming in. I remember turning in my pager the day I left. The project manager wanted me to keep it "in case he needed to call me", never mind the company wasn't paying me anymore. I was on the stairs walking out and he tossed the pager to me. I made no attempt to catch it and the pager clattered down the stairwell. As I walked on down the stairs to where it lay, I gave it a hell of a kick. Our division had made over $300 million dollars that year, but the other division ran by a know-nothing yuppie who had made never ending mistakes, with full knowledge of most of the upper managers, lost much more. The owner of the company was busy drinking in a local Newport Beach bar from noon to five daily and couldn't be bothered. The mangers wouldn't take action and because of it, lots of good people lost their livelihoods, for no reason other than pitifully bad management. The good ship I was on, just sank with no warning.

I realized I had to find a job quickly to stay "afloat". I saw an ad in the paper and realized, even though they didn't print their name, who the company was, and made an all out effort to get the job that was offered.

Over 150 people applied for the job and I got it. I did some major sucking up to get it, but hell, I needed a pay check. Over the next few years, the recession that had begun before I was hired, deepened. One day, all the employees of the company were called to the Shilo Hotel for a meeting. Just the name of the hotel was ominous. At a place called Shilo in the Civil War, a battle was fought and a lot of people died. We were told a new deal was coming our way. We were going to build zero defect homes. We were all going to become better at our jobs and we were going to be a better company. Sounded good.

Soon thereafter, we were all issued daily planners and asked to come in and take a day to learn how to use them. The guy was a great speaker. The planner seemed to be a great tool and I later found out it was better than I thought.

Over the next few months, we'd have meeting after meeting to get our company to function so we could build homes with absolutely no defects. I was put in charge of the process of writing a checklist to do just that. It worked. We did it... We were so good at building houses, we completely eliminated a whole customer service department. We did it...but there was a problem. The guy who came out regularly, would sit in meetings and say, "Everyone has got it around here, excepting the people at the management level. If you don't change at the corporate level, then this will not work long term. If the corporate people don't change, then in time, the company will fall back into where they were before we started the transformation." Bottom line, we worker bees were with the program, but the guys in charge, weren't changing and didn't plan to change. They had things the way they liked them and weren't going to change.

Along with the daily planners came changes. There were several people that were fired, thrown overboard to the sharks. Some were very good at their jobs. The recession was on and finding a good job wasn't easy. There was an element of fear in the company. If you didn't do all "the new things right", you could get fired. A list of the company's commandments was printed and distributed. One of the items on the list was "No Mavericks". In construction, you have to have a lot of Mavericks.

Finally, one day, I decided I'd rather just get back in the water with the sharks. Before I left, I wrote "The Galley" and gave it to one of the purchasing gals to read. I never understood why a construction company would make a woman a purchasing agent, knowing the gal had never dug a ditch, never roofed a house, never ran a piece of equipment, and for sure never poured any concrete, but they do. She never got "The Galley" either, but I'll always have the satisfaction of knowing, from time to time, she just might stop and pause and wonder if there was any real message in "The Galley" she may have missed.

Steve Richey

The ocean was vast, stretching from horizon to horizon in every direction. The sun was relentless in its searing heat. A young man was treading the deep blue water hoping a ship would come close enough to pick him up and save his life. He had been in the water for a long time and he knew that he couldn't last much longer.

He had recently been on a fine ship, sound and sea-worthy. He was happy with his life. He made enough money to support his family and was thought of well by his friends and neighbors. The time he spent on his ship was a fair price to pay for the life he lived. All that changed in a few hours one day.

His ship was routinely sailing along and suddenly began taking on water. In a few hours it sank. A few of the officers were able to get into life boats but he and many others soon found themselves swimming all alone in the ocean, with nothing to cling to. His will to stay alive was strong, so he fought to keep his head above water, but time was passing and in time, he knew his strength would fail. He found a piece of driftwood he could drape his arms over and stay afloat, but still he knew he desperately needed to get out of the water. His only hope was to find another ship in this vast ocean and get on board.

As the deep blue waves picked him up and lifted him to their crest, he could see other men, just like himself across the ocean, treading water, also hoping for a passing ship to pick them up. Occasionally someone would pass near enough to talk to for a few moments, which was very good, but all too soon they would separate. Often, he would see someone slip beneath the surface and disappear forever. He felt so very alone and in a hopeless situation.

Early one morning, as a wave crested, he caught a glimpse of what appeared to be the tip of a sail on the horizon, possibly the mast of a ship. His body was immediately filled with hope and a new energy. When the next wave lifted him, he saw it was indeed a sail. A ship! The next wave to lift him, allowed him to see the ship. It looked as if it were coming in his direction. Hope became desperation. To live, he had to get on that ship!

At the crest of each wave, the mast of the ship became larger, with more sail visible, then finally he could see men on the deck of the ship. As the ship came closer he could see it was a merchant galley. It had a single fairly large sail, but on both sides of the ship, rows of long oars reached out into the water. He could hear the methodical beating of a large hammer on a hollowed log inside the ship, setting the rhythm of the galley slaves to row by. He knew inside the ship were men, chained to their oars, most of them for a lifetime of hard work, but still, they were alive. He knew if he got on that ship, he most likely would be there for the rest of his life but he also knew alone in the water, he could not survive much longer. He was lucky the sharks had not attacked him already. He had the choice to stay in the water and die or hopefully live by getting on the ship, if only they would pick him up. He chose life and swam toward the oncoming ship.

The ship came closer. He could hear the splashing of the oars, the methodical rowing beat, and an occasional snap of a whip as a driver lashed out at a tired oar slave. He was now along side the ship and he yelled, "Ahoy On Deck! Bring me on board!"

A man glared over the railing and yelled, "Why should we?!"

"I'm strong and young, I can be of value to you for years to come!" the young man yelled.

"So you say," the man yelled back with a grin on his face.

"I'll work double shifts and I don't eat much!" yelled the young man. The ship was nearly half way past him.

"Have you had much experience?" yelled the deck hand.

"Not a lot, but I learn quickly!" frantically yelled the young man. The ship was now nearly passed.

Suddenly, there was a large splash in the water at the stern of the ship and an old exhausted rower bobbed in the water for a moment and sank below the surface.

"We've just now had an opening!" yelled the man above with a smile on his face, then threw the young man a rope. The young man climbed the rope with all the strength he had left.

He dragged himself over the railing and collapsed on the warm deck. Being out of the water felt so good to him. He felt the solid deck under him and the sun on his legs and thought, "I'm no longer in deep water and I'm on a ship! The sharks can't get me here." Life had taken a turn for the better for him.

"Here now, that won't do," said the man who had thrown him a rope so he could climb on board. The young man looked at him and realized the deck hand was actually a pudgy officer of the ship. "It's rowing you said you were good for so down below with you now. You'll row a shift, we'll call it a probationary period, and then you can rest. This isn't a luxury barge you know. You do well on your shift and we'll find something for you to eat and drink."

The officer motioned for two men to come over. They roughly picked the young up man by the arms and dragged him across the deck then down a hatch into the belly of the ship. The men dragged the young man into the rowing galley where a hundred or more men were straining at their oars, pulling to the beater's beat. What air there was, was saturated with a level of foulness never before experienced by the young man, having the effect of smelling salts, jolting him alert.

He was dragged to a seat and plopped down on it. The men fastened an iron leg bracelet to his ankle then threaded a chain through a ring on the bracelet and finally locked the end of the chain to an eye hook near the aisle.

He found himself seated next to a leathery old man. The old man's skin was like dried cowhide. He was thin and sinuous. He had a long beard, rough hands, and little hair on his head. His dark leather skin of his face made his violet blue eyes shine like two deep blue halogen headlights.

One of the guards sternly told him to "Row to the beat" and walked off. The young man grabbed his oar and began to strain at it. The beater continued to beat a steady beat as the rowers rowed.

Whomp	Row
Whomp	Row
Whomp	Row

The old man was watching him and then spoke in a gravely voice, "New rower are you now?"

"Yeah, I got lucky. Just got hauled out of the sea. Couldn't have lasted much longer out there. No food, bad water, and there were plenty of sharks too."

"My name is Old Man. Yours?" said the old man as he leaned into a stroke, arms stretched away from his body, his callused hands grasping the oar and his unchained foot, pushing off on the seat in front of him, using his whole body to pull the oar through the water.

"Son," said the young man.

"Watch me row Son," said the old man. "You need to use your whole body to last the shift.

Relax. Breathe. Rowing on this ship, you'll need to use your brains also. They don't hesitate to throw you back in if you don't pull to the beat," cautioned the old man.

"Thanks for the warning. I appreciate you giving me good advice," said Son. "How long you been rowing on this ship?"

"Bout five years," said the old man.

"How is it on this ship," Son asked.

"Good as any I suppose, better than most really. We eat fairly regular. They don't beat us that often. We have to work extra shifts now and then due to the recession. It's hard times these days. We don't have the extra rowers we used to have. Do your job, row to the beat, do as your asked when you're asked and you can get along. You're young. They throw a lot of us old timers overboard. I have to worry about that. They have a retirement plan, but few rowers ever get to use it. If the guys above are feeling good, they'll dump you off on some island, rather than throw you over-board in deep water. Most of the time when they want someone gone, they aren't near land. A guy will get thrown overboard bout the time they near retirement. It's the recession economics most corporations and galleys follow you know. They'll dump you overboard rather than see you reach retirement. Just row steady. You can last a good while."

*   *   *   *   *

several weeks later…. The recession had deepened….

Whomp   Row
Whomp   Row
Whomp   Row

"Hey, Old Man, how's it going. I haven't been
chained next to you for a shift in several weeks.
How ya been?"

"Rowing to the beat, just like everyone here
Son," smiled the Old Man.

"Have you heard about the big change com'n
Old Man. Don't know yet what it will be, but the
officers say we'll like it. Some guy is gonna talk to
us soon. He's coming out on a private boat from
another corporation. One of those corporations
that show up when recessions deepen and I hear
they help keep your boats afloat. He's gonna talk
to us rowers. Could be things will get better."

"Well Son, there's always hope. Hope pops up each day just like the sun does. Even when it's cloudy, the sun shines above the clouds and hope is always there. Things don't always change for the worse. We'll most likely get to put our oars down for a while to listen to him, but you can count on as soon as he leaves, we'll have to pick up the pace to make up for the distance we lost while we listened to the man talk. If the change makes things for the better I'll row to it, but we'll row to the beat what-ever it is. That's the way of the ship you know. Row to the ship's beat or get throw'd overboard."

Later on that day, a man did come on board. Son could see him up through the deck hatch openings. He was well dressed, but was a weasely looking type guy. He seemed energetic and full of purpose. He shook hands with all the guys above deck and had something to say to each one of them, lots of laughing and his head was bobbing up and down. When he had finished, he then came down to the rowing galley.

He walked down the center aisle looking at each rower. He had a whole team of people with him, all dressed up, pretty much alike. These people had charts and graphs on them, which they passed out to all the rowers. He then stepped up on a rowing block on the first row and began to speak. He spoke well and used fine words, but he had a bad speaking problem. When he spoke, he spit back at least two rows. The rowers directly in front of him had to keep bobbing and weaving as he talked to keep from being spit on.

The man talked of "waste". You eliminate waste, you increase productivity, get better results. It was a good speech, made sense, and when he left, we only had to pick up the speed for another 6 hours. We all had a good laugh at the boys in the front row getting spit on. They were looking like punchy ex-boxers up there while being talked to, bobbing and weaving, trying to keep from being spit on.

*   *   *   *

The next day…….

"That guy sounded pretty good to me yester-day. What do you think of what he said?" Son asked the Old Man?

"Well Son, you're new around here. It takes a while to change the speed and course of something as large as this ship. It will be a little unsteady and uncertain for a while until we all learn to pull together at the same time. With the new deal, we'll have to learn a new rhythm I'm sure. The guy didn't sound too bad, but then again, we're just starting down this road. Time will tell if it's a good road or has lots of ruts in it.

There isn't much room allowed for the differ-ence in rowers in the new deal. Some of us take a little longer strokes and make up for the shorter armed guys. It averages and works out pretty well. The new system though, dictates everyone has to row exactly the same stroke. Humans are all different. Corporations don't allow much for human differences. If your natural rhythm is the new standard stroke, then you'll adjust easily. A little guy though, will have to work harder to pull the new stroke and guys like me, who tend to pull a longer stroke, will have to adjust to the standard stroke. Lots of us will have to change and not all those changes will be better for the ship. If you're a little faster or slower than the standard stroke, you'll have to struggle with it."

The Old Man spoke on, as he pulled on his oar. "The check list they talked about. It's a way to measure and standardize each of our strokes, but it won't be easy to get everyone to row the same stroke. Ain't much room for the human factor in this new rhythm. This rule #10 that says, "No Mavericks". That a warning son. It's saying you have to row the same stroke every time and you'll be checked on it. If you don't do the standard stroke exactly, you probably won't be long for the ship."

"Take me for example. I row hardest just before a storm when the wind freshens or as we go into battle. With the new deal, I won't be allowed to do that. I'll have to row the standard stroke, day in and day out, come'n a rain or going into battle… every time, all the time. What they need is a good diesel engine that strokes the same every time and they can control the speed by the amount of fuel given to the engine. They could replace us rowers with engines, but engines haven't been invented yet and that's probably a good thing. If they had diesels we'd all be shark bait. It'd be just like all the American companies that give all their work to Mexico and India and China. As soon as their work goes south or overseas, they throw their workers overboard. Don't need them anymore."

"The new standardized stroke should be fairly easy to master," said Son. They have a checklist for each part of the stroke:

I.   bend forward

II.   right foot on the seat in front of you

III.   push off with your right foot

IV.   arms straight

V.   lean back and pull on your oar

VI.   push with both feet

VII. lean back as far as you can
VIII. pull the oar to your chest while leaning back
IX. push your oar down to your waist
X. bend your knees and learn forward to 1 position.

None of it sounds too hard. It even has a checklist of how to recover when you get lashed with the whip. It has some good advice on how to heal whip marks, how to keep going in a long shift, and how to heal blisters. It's not a bad check list."

Old Man looked at Son and quietly said, "The checklist is a way to perform the standard stroke sure, but it's also a way to measure each man's output, to make sure you're putting out at least the required minimum they need you to. As different as we all are, they want all of us to produce the same with absolute predictability. That's the reason for Clause #10 in the New Ship's orders, "No Mavericks".

"Never thought of that," Son said pensively. "This checklist thing then is more for them to get more out of us, than help us do better then?"

"I think that may be so," said Old Man. " I believe they're fixing to reduce the rowers. If they can get us to believe the new deal is a good idea, do the work of more than one man, they can begin to throw some of us overboard, and that will cut their operation costs...which will increase their profits. The ship will get to their markets in the same time with the standardized strokes and it will cost less to get there, because there are fewer of us to feed...or will be as soon as they begin to throw anyone they feel like overboard. If they can get to the market, with less cost, they can sell their merchandise at a reduced price, and still keep the same profit margin.... It's economics Son, pure economics."

Old Man took a deep breath, leaned into his stroke and went on. "Of course, the guys above deck could cut the commissions down for the peddlers that sell our goods or get the peddlers to stop throwing in so much free merchandise on deals to get the sale. That would help a lot to increase profits and keep a few of us from being thrown overboard. Most buyers would close the deal without so much baksheesh.

Merchants don't buy our goods Son, they buy what our goods will do for them. The only two reasons the merchants buy are to solve a problem or to resell what we sell them and make profit for themselves. The reason they show up to the stalls with our merchandise is they've been to the stalls of the other peddlers and decided our stalls will satisfy their needs at the least cost. They want to buy from us. They're gonna buy from us. The only real undecided question the buyers have is how much baksheesh they can manipulate our peddlers to throw in for free.

"Baksheesh… What's that Old Man?"

"That's stuff you throw in to entice the buyers to close the deal. Baksheesh can be a few more items of what they are buying, some cash given back to the buyer, maybe a hoochie momma or two, can be a camel, it all depends on the size of the buyers purchase and how much anxiety the peddler has about losing the deal." said the Old Man.

"Isn't that good business?" asked Son

"Ain't good business son when you drop the prices on goods, throw in a lot of baksheesh that costs our owners cash to buy, and then pay the "good times" rate of commission on the sale of the goods to the peddlers. The money left over is supposed to make a profit for the owners of the ship, buy more goods here to take to the next port, keep the ship in good repairs, and buy food for us rowers", said Old Man.

"So, Old Man, what your saying is the peddlers have dropped their prices on our goods, are giving away expensive baksheesh to close the deal, and are still getting the same rate of commission today, as they were getting in the past good times?" asked Son is a wide eyed look of disbelief.

"Yep" said Old Man. "No matter how fast we get the goods to market, we're losing all our profits due to high bonuses paid to our peddlers and the lower price the same peddlers are selling our goods at."

"The new deal will change all that, don't you think Old Man?" asked Son

"Hard to say Son. None of us have been thrown overboard lately, but we're working the new deal, and I don't see much change for the better. We just have to wait and see. New deals take time to evaluate." Said Old man.

Six months later…the beat had been picked up.

Whomp	Row
Whomp	Row
Whomp	Row

"Hey Old Man. How do you like the new beat?" asked Son.

"I'm cutting it Son. They've thrown some guys overboard. I notice every once in a while, another seat empty. See all those empty rowing blocks where there used to be rowers."

"Wow! I hadn't noticed. I've been so intent on doing the standard stroke, trying to do it just like the checklist." said Son.

"They could be picking up guys to fill the seats. They're plenty of men out there in the sea. They pass under my oars every day. The Captain had one of our guys make some nice signs to hang all over the place. I really like the one that says, "Give them more than they expect." It's really got a nice ring to it, but then again, I haven't figured out whom it's for yet. Probably for some of the customers up top we are rowing to the next port. One thing for sure, the peddlers have got that one down pat. Would be nice if the guys above the deck could see below deck. We can't eat signs you know."

"Are you feeling any stress from the new beat Old Man?" asked Son.

"Well, ha...ha... I was a little and then to reduce my stress, the guys above deck got me this here new daily planner. It's supposed to help me get it together and make me more efficient. Did you get one too Son?"

"Sure did. It's nice and shiney and new, but I can't figure out how to put my oar down long enough to write in it Old Man. You got any ideas of how to fill in the pages?" asked Son.

"Do what I do Son. When you get off shift, write in it then...make sure you do, be seen doing it, fill in all your pages. It's very important to have the guys above deck believe you're totally going for their program. Remember the clause #10, "No Mavericks". Some of those thrown overboard recently didn't fill in their planner."

"But that's the time I get to doctor my blisters and whip marks. Then's when I get to talk to the other rowers about their shifts and talk about when we used to get to see our families....and sleep...and enjoy life," said Son as he shook his head despondently.

"Son, see what I'm setting on. I have my daily

planner under me all during my shift and next to me
at all times. You should too. Don't pay to be non-
standard these days. Look out that oar hole. Do
you see all them guys out there in the deep, deep
sea, tread'n water, wanting to get on our ship? If'n
they don't find a ship soon Son, sharks'll get'm for
sure. You need to practice your standard stroke
Son, be seen with your daily planner, smile a lot,
and say damn little. It don't take nothin for the
Cap'n to throw a guy overboard these days. You
might be lucky enough to catch another ship, you
might not. Just you keep thinking bout those
sharks out there. That'll motivate you to find time
to use that daily planner. Keep it filled up! They'll
pick them up one day and give you another. It'd
better be full of good words about the ship and a
few extra pages to boot. Do as I tell you now.
Times aren't good and as bad as it is here, it can get
a hell of a lot worse in the snap of your fingers, out
there in the ocean along with everyone else that
don't have a ship!"

*   *   *   *   *

Two months later…the beat had been increased again.

Whomp………Row…………Whomp…………Row

Whomp………Row…………Whomp…………Row

Whomp………Row…………Whomp…………Row

Son was brought to his oar and chained to his rowing block. Old man was on his block, rowing to the beat.

"Hey Old Man, you ain't looking so good…" said Son.

"Little weary, I am Son...little weary....this new beat is getting to me..." sighed Old Man.

"Your stroke seems standard.... You're sitting on your daily planner... Do you go through all the daily checklists each day...before, during, and after your shift?" asked Son. "The guys above deck say that's supposed to help a lot. The guy from the east coast that's helping us with the new deal says so too, and he ought to know. He **told** us he's an **expert** didn't he!" said Son.

"Yeah...he' told us son...but is he? I used to just stroke to the beat...now I gotta stroke, do check lists, work on teams to improve our strokes...takes a lot of time this new deal. I see a lot of fear in people. We all still have the same ship to row the same distance to market, but now with all the new deal work, we have less time at the oars to get us there and we have fewer rowers." Sighed Old Man.

"I've been hearing about all the good work you been doing Old Man. You've been on lots of committees. The guys above deck gotta love you!" said Son encouragingly.

"Son, do you think they know or even care? I have my doubts. When's the last time one came to your oar and told you what a great improvement you've made or gave you a little time away from your oar during you shift because they appreciate you? Is your food gett'n any better? Mine sure ain't. Ain't that the same block you've been rowing at before the guy from the east came out and started this new deal? Not much has changed with your block or oar. Have you had time to go up above deck and see the sun lately? I didn't think so. Me either… same for all of us. This deal was never designed for us Son."

Old Man went on…. "Hell Son, I never even see the guys above deck anymore. They used to come down here and beat us every now and then.

I wasn't all that glad to see'm, but while they were beating us, they were screaming at you and telling you what they expected. Anymore, they're in meetings all the time with this new deal. A negative painful encounter was better than no encounter and no communication. Never seeing them makes your mind wander and start to think about when they're gonna pick up the beat on us again of if you're gonna be the next one throw'd overboard. This standard stroke and lists and daily planner I'm sittin' on could be doing wonders, but the guys above deck can't see any of it if'n they're in meetings all the time and if'n I'm here at my oar day after day after day. I sure can't see anything changing for the better.

I was on top the other day in a meeting and noticed some of the guys above deck were missing. They probably jumped ship the last port we were in. The guys above deck get more news than we do and when they start jumping ship, then it's a sure sign of hard times. We'll be seeing some new faces above deck before long, looking down the hatches at us. They usually come on board and begin to make changes, so's to look as if they are earning their keep, but it's usually at our expense. To get their jobs, they've had to convince the ship's owners they can make a profit where others couldn't. I'd store a little food if I were you while we're getting what we're getting. The new guys will most likely pick up the beat and cut down on the rations or men at the oars to produce higher profits. They always expect us rowers to make their promises good. We're expendable. These are uncertain times Son."

"Old Man, you're looking very thin and worn. Is there any way I can help?" asked Son softly.

"Thanks Son. You're a good oar mate. I do appreciate your offer, but you can't handle your oar and mine too. Hopefully we'll reach a better market soon. I figure as soon as the market picks up, the guys above deck will turn into the guys they used to be. This new deal will only last as long as the market is bad and everyone is scrambling to not get thrown in the sea. Some of the guys above deck get thrown in from time to time also. They usually get a life jacket at the worst, some get a small boat, but still, it's a big ocean.

The owners have other ships that sail to different ports and better markets. When the market is better and the profits are better, the owners will treat the guys above deck very differently. What the owners and all the guys above deck are doing now is a way of structuring their time until they're making good profits again and that will come when the economy changes. Soon as we get to better markets and better profits, everyone's conditions will get better and they'll all forget this new deal. Until then, I'll just row my standard stroke, to their beat, keep my daily planner warm, watch all those guys out there with the sharks, and smile... smile....smile.... Where I am is much better than out there with the sharks!"

"Speaking of guys out there with the sharks...there seems to be more of them out there lately.." said Son.

"Yep," said Old Man. "Was talking to a new rower the other day. We're one of the few ships afloat in this ocean. Lots and lots of rowers out there Son. Don't miss a beat...."

*　　　*　　　*　　　*　　　*

A month later the guy from the east coast came on board. The rowers were all stopped while he gave them a tremendously uplifting motivational speech. He was so excited he spit about four rows back instead of his usual two rows. He talked to them about all kinds of things like wasted effort, time commitments, supporting the guys above deck, then he hit on the "No Mavericks" pretty hard. He finished his speech then went up on deck for a big dinner and a party with some hoochie mommas he had brought with him. Guys like him and hoochie mommas seemed to have a lot in common. As soon as he went topside..the beat picked up again.

Whomp......Row....Whomp....Row....Whomp....
...Row...Whomp....Row

Whomp......Row....Whomp....Row....Whomp....
...Row...Whomp....Row

Son sat down beside Old Man for his shift...
"Jeez Old Man, you're looking really bad!"

"…………   "Can't   make……..it   much longer…………with this new beat," groaned Old Man, pulling at his oar, flopping back in exhausting to position #1.

"I know," said Son. "I feel like I'm in an endless workout movie!"

"Hey…..that's   funny Son…..Hah……….Hah………Hah……."

"Glad to see you still have a sense of humor Old Man. Lots of us have lost ours. Remember when we used to get together and we'd all talk an laugh. Now we just get together in quiet groups. We're all scarred," said Son.

"It's just....the psycho.....social......paradign......" said Old Man.

"What's that?" asked Son.

"People's actions reflecting their circumstances Son," said Old Man.

"Never thought about it Old Man, but now that I do, you're right. You sure are smart Old Man."

"Nah Son......our......oars.....are ....the .....same....length....." panted Old Man.

"That guy from the east. He's due back in a month. Every time he shows up, they take time out of our shifts and pick up the beat as soon as he goes topside. Ten to one, he'll show up and they'll pick up the beat..." said Son.

"I.....can't........row.....any.......faster....Son I.....just.....can't." said Old Man in a state of exhaustion and near collapse.

*   *   *   *   *

One month later…the guy from the east came back and the beat picked up while he was giving his motivation speech instead of after. The guys didn't even get to put down their oars while he was talking.

Whomp..Row..Whomp..Row..Whomp..Row..
Whomp..Row..Whomp..Row..Whomp..Row..
Whomp..Row..Whomp..Row..Whomp..Row..

Early the next day, Son was once again led to his rowing block and locked in. He looked to his left and there was a new rower there. As soon as the chain man left Son looked at the new oarman and said, "Hey…who are you? That's Old Man's oar! Where is he?!"

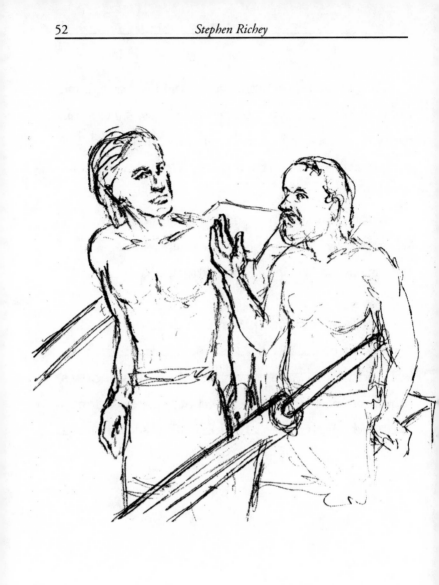

"Gone. You must be Son."

"I am," Son said. "Gone where, to another oar...working the bilge pumps...where is Old Man?"

"He's not on this ship anymore..." said the new rower.

"The bastards, they threw him over, didn't they.....they picked up the beat until he couldn't keep up with the standard stroke and then threw him overboard...didn't they! They used him up and then threw him to the sharks!" Son said with a cold blooded anger in his eyes.

"No, they didn't get the chance Son. Old Man, he was a smart one. He left on his own. He took that plastic flap out of his daily planner and made it into a key. Picked his lock, he did, and got away. He's a free man now. He had it all figured out.."

"Figured out....but where'd he go...I don't understand," said Son.

"Well, you know the guys above deck never come down here anymore where the works being done. Old Man counted on that," said the new man. He then continued on, "Old Man took all those check lists and with a lot of'm, he made a board he could stand on that would float....water proofed it with some of the greasy food we get daily so's it wouldn't get soggy and made it hollow so's the center would hold fresh water. He then took more check lists, you know we got so many of them there's always plenty around....and he made a tall pole and again used the greasy food as glue and water proofing. He took more and made a sail. He took the binder rings of his daily planner and hooked one to the foot of the sail....then slipped the rest of the rings over the tall pole he made. He made a socket in the board that would hold the pole. He made a keel out of his planner's hard covers and fastened it to the bottom of his board. He even took those clear pouches in the planner and put a couple in the middle of his sail, so's he could see where he was going. He called the thing a wind surfer. He got it all done and shoved it out through his oar hole after unlocking his shackle with the key he had made. He'd lost so much weight from the faster beats, he put some of that greasy food on his body, and squeezed right out through the oar hole in a wink.

He then took one end of the pole and after slipping the sail over it, plunked it down in the center hole he'd made. He had taken some cloth, ripped it into strips, and wove some line, then attached the line to one end of the sail…so he could control the wind and steer with it.

He looked so great, out there in the sunset…his hair blowing in the wind…he looked a foot taller out there than he did at his oar. Said he was head'n for the Isle of Santosha. I watched him sail off myself, I did. Nobody top side saw him. They were in a meeting. I tell you, t'was a sight I'll never forget…Old Man out there standing on that board, the wind carrying him away, the sun making the ocean look all orange and warm…Old Man, he'll make it."

"I'm gonna miss him," Son said sadly.

"You don't have to you know Son. He said were I ever to row next to you I was to give you a message…"

"Really….what was Old Man's message to me," asked Son eagerly.

"Old Man said to remind you, you too have a planner…. and in the planner, you'll always find the key….

The end.

Printed in the United States
106331LV00001B/112-159/A